T0129508

Printed in the United States
By Bookmasters

Carnality:

The Spiritual Matrix

SUSAN HORTON

authorHOUSE®

AuthorHouse™
1663 Liberty Drive
Bloomington, IN 47403
www.authorhouse.com
Phone: 1-800-839-8640

Published by AuthorHouse   11/1/2012

ISBN: 9-781-4772-8644-9 (sc)
ISBN: 9-781-4772-8797-2 (e)

Library of Congress Control Number: 2012920726

This is for all those who see
outside of the journey and are
experiencing true enlightenment.

The seekers are finding
e lost are being found
eary has found rest
e physicians are
ng themselves!

In the beginning…

This is how all of our stories start. Once upon a time is just another way of saying the very same thing. Beginnings have different props and backdrops but every single one of our lives began "in the beginning". Darwinism has nothing on Genesis 1:1.

"In the beginning, God Created…" is more than just a bible verse; it is a blueprint for how we are to structure our lives. We see where God saw a purpose and began creating. It was just that simple. He saw the turmoil the earth was in…I believe the exact words were null and void. Nothing and empty, that's how we all started out. As a groom prepares a home for his new bride, He formed the layers of the atmosphere and from each he comprised the earths' shape, he set the planets in motion and called it "good".

Jah then began calling forth the dry ground, exposing the mountains, the rocks, the volcanoes and the caves. He decided to decorate each plain, plateau, isthmus, and island with all types of plant life. The part of HIM that is feminine, began to beautify the face of the earth, immaculately placing every bush in its perspective climate and saw that is was good. Elohim, being the sportsman that he is, saw a purpose for wildlife. He began forming tiny personas in the forms of animals. He carefully fashioned the food chain and gave each animal instructions on how he was to maintain the cycle of life. Some were created for everyday uses, such as food and clothing, but others were strategically placed to impress the love of His existence. Tropical fish, birds like cockatoos and toucans, or even the flowers and trees that are pleasing to the eyes, but aren't apart of the food chain are the marks of duality in the DEITY as we know it. She was pleased and called them good.

After they did a quick inventory and saw that all was in place, they scooped up a handful of clay and began fashioning a dress for their new bride's arrival. They opened the door by inhaling and then exhaling into the frame of Their most prized possession… man. Again, Jehovah grinned sheepishly, because all this was to please Their greatest creation to date. God named him Adam. Like any proud father/mother would, God took his tiny twin around and showed him all that he created and then gave him the charge to name and put each in its place. The earth and the fullness thereof were for this lord's pleasure, the whole world and they that dwell therein.

God saw that god was not savoring his new digs. He was still longing for a deeper connection. This god was lonely, just as the GOD before him. So They did just what They did for Themselves. They put god to sleep, not to deter any pain or suffering, but because They wanted to surprise him with this special gift. They (GOD) then began separating all that was lovely, nurturing, beautiful, intuitive, meticulous, sensitive, passionate, and insightful and lay it beside god. He (god) then opened his eyes and saw that it was good. He said I will call her woman (me with a chalice). GOD, god and goddess lived happily ever after. Who knew things wouldn't just keep getting better.

Man/Woman
(god/goddess)

Some would say it is sacra-religious for me to refer to man as god. In all actuality this is the correct interpretation of who men & women are. They are small images of the great GOD who created him. When GOD began creating and finished fashioning the world we live in, He exclaimed "Let *us* make man". This "us" that many have theorized about is the duality that is us. HE/SHE is the all consuming, all knowing, all seeing; everlasting GOD that created the god/goddess that is us. Many scientists believe that we were formed from a large mass that exploded and in that mass explosion are the particles that govern who we are. Isn't this the perfect explanation of what birth is? Our births can best be described as an explosion resulting in the makeup of our human anatomy. We are actually stars, not Hollywood publicity jocks, but luminescent matter that glow and give off warmth. We are small planets that are individual personalities; productions of our Creators vivid imagination.

It is carnality that won't allow us to believe that we are more than we are and it is carnality that keeps us fighting with our natural ascension to submit to another's. We have the ability to transcend our physical bodies and travel the outer reaching perimeters of the Milky Way without even leaving the ground. Enoch and Elisha showed us that walking with GOD will allow us to experience life as it was designed in Eden.

Enoch walked with God.

Elisha did not pass thru the portal of death but was whisked away.

Truth is the ritual of doing something makes it more real. The Baptists, the Methodists, the Masons, the Eastern stars, the Protestants, the Jews, the Muslims and even wiccans all have orders of service that makes each organization different, but because each has the tool of ritualism they are the same. Nothing makes it real except a belief in what it is you are doing. The only qualifications Jesus asked of us is simply to believe that He is and we could be saved. Tongues, tarrying, fasting, rolling on the floor, passing out….they give the people around you something to talk about, but not a lot happens in the spirit realm. "Upon this rock I will build my church…" the entity of blind faith is this solid foundation that Jesus would establish this new order of service. The only way to participate is to lose sight of labels, conditions, limitations, prejudices, misunderstandings, partialities, frailties, shortcomings, and traditions. Peter walked on water because he didn't give in to the laws of physics. Jesus told him to come because he saw Peter's capacity to believe beyond the labels. That blind faith caused him to walk on that which was consuming.

He became buoyant in the sinkable because those conditions did not dictate his faith. Carnality is the death that man/woman died in that garden when the fruit of disobedience was exercised by Adam. We lost our deity and settled for a confining, finite existence all for the participation in what we already possessed. Ego tricked us into seeing past what we already had in our beings to what was Adam thinking when he saw the result of consuming or ingesting this line of thinking?

Ego is the fuel that drives carnality. It is that feeling that drives you to be right or to defend that which doesn't deserve defending. Everyone has an ego. When god (Adam) consumed the fruit and blamed (goddess) Eve for causing him to stumble, ego was the emotion that he was feeling when he blamed her for his disobedience. GOD gave the command to him, and left it to his discretion to inform her of its consequences. Ego was the feeling that drove her to follow the instructions of someone who is influencing her to do something that she believes is suspect. What a dolt this goddess was when she gave the serpent place in her psyche. We do the exact same thing when we submit our spiritual esteem to the influence of another. We shrink down into a death of inability when we allow someone else's ego to cause us to stumble.

Ego has been here since the Great Architect fashioned our world. It was first introduced to us in the form of the serpent. The serpent or as it is commonly known, the snake, although created by GOD was the one urging us to temptation of knowledge. It was not the actual act but the introduction to our subconscious which is the home for our baser instincts such as carnality, jealousy, idolatry, and greed which are all enmity again GOD. HE/SHE will not remove temptation from our path, but will provide a way of escaping its snare. He is patiently waiting for us to return to a more developed sense of consciousness. In other words, HE/SHE causes us to triumph. We are designed to win, but we must at least acknowledge the existence of ego in its defeated position.

We are experiencing a terrible time in finances, the earth's atmosphere, and local tragedies because we are spiritually in a deficit. We are not living the life carefully crafted for us when HE designed Eden. You know the only difference between then and now is our attitude. As I have said and will repeat throughout this book, we have been restored to our original sinless state via Jesus. The only thing keeping up from enjoying it is our mind's eye being clouded with the cares and labels from this world.

Labels are the shades we paint the world according to our experiences. We have called good people and things bad and vice versa, all because of how we relate to them. We have created a one dimensional existence. So my friend whether you have accepted the title or not, you are a god and creation is your inheritance. It is up to you to decide what destiny you will choose. You can choose to have a life of freedom and power or be a victim with finite vision and no joy.

The letter killeth, but Jesus came to make the word 3D. Some of you are reading this right now and disagreeing with every word I have typed, but you live lawlessly and have no spiritual structure to your existence. You have not maintained your allotment and are sitting there judging me for trying to inspire those who will. Carnality is the wool pulled over our spiritual eyes that blinds us from the truth Christ died for. Truth of the matter is He came so that we could be restored to our rightful place in the kingdom. He is now the portal to which we can return to Eden...even if we happen to be living in New Jersey!

We are plugged into a system that drains all of our energy and forces us to dwell in the subconscious realm. What we must strive to attain is a merging once again of the conscience and the subconscious. This balance is only produced when we understand that all the tangible things like "feelings" and labels are links in a chain that confines us to this reality and makes it difficult for us to accept our deity. Jesus' efforts will be in vain if we don't grasp that His dissension and ascension was purely so that we could receive restoration and begin the journey back to Eden.

We allow our imagination too much space in our everyday lives. If something is not how we want it to be in the real world, we will fix it by giving it all it is missing in our minds. This plays into the system of thought that we are the constructors of our own fate. If Eve had not been caught up in her imagination, she would have been conscious of the law. She was creating the perfect world of having brought this perfect fruit to her husband and having his approval and denying the conditions with which she could abide in a paradise that had already been carefully established for them both.

Let's look at Adam and Eve; not as people but as the conscious and subconscious minds. Adam will be the conscious because the law was explained to him about the tree of the knowledge of good and evil so the morality and obedience of its constitution was solely on him. Here comes Eve; the subconscious or whimsical, and emotionally motivated mind. Had these two known each other or become one before the partaking of the tree of the knowledge of good and evil, then the conscious mind could have subdued the subconscious mind and the fall may have been prevented. Now had that happened then there would have been no need for Calvary. Since the separating of morality and emotionalism caused a void in our lives, there is an overwhelming urgency for God's grace via Jesus' sacrifice.

God
(Man's Misunderstanding)

Spiritual Rehabilitation:

After a very powerful deliverance service on any given Sunday and God showed out the way HE is known to show out, we leave our respective edifices on a spiritual high. This is partly because we are experiencing the emotional release and then again, we are amongst a different element. We have made the decision to live this life finally and nothing can keep us from this joy. Before we leave the grounds however, our dissension back into the spiritual matrix begins and this is how the scenario is played out:

Sunday we leave church on that high, so much so our feet aren't even touching the ground. It doesn't matter that Deacon Knock-Knees has cut us off in the parking lot because we remember that God locked the wheels of our enemies chariots or at least in his case we are hoping God lets the air out of one of those may pop tires he riding on. But it's all good… it's all good. We turn up our favorite Marvin Sapp song 'Never would have made it' and we weep all the way home thinking of the word God just ministered to us when the phone rings. Its sister Stacey…you know she's calling to gossip, so you press the ignore button and lift your hands because of this small triumph. By Sunday evening we may have cussed out our husband or kids, but it's ok because we still haven't touched down just yet.

Monday morning…we are up before the alarm rings! We are still energized from that emotional release that took place at the altar that sends us back into a tearfully grateful state so we spend some time on our knees… not really praying, because we are preoccupied with so many other things but it was a valiant effort. The alarm goes off and we are off! The children are up and hubby still can't get dressed without you. You spend all your time dressing them until you don't have enough left for yourself. You said you were going to get some gas on the way to work but there was an unexpected accident which threw you behind about 30 min. Now this is your third warning and you say to yourself, "Devil I know this is you, like my co-pastor says, get the behind me…SHUT UP!!!…in the mighty name of Jesus!"

We get into the office and we see Stacy standing by the water cooler and we go the other way thinking, that we have changed and the devil will not be my influence. She corners us before we make it to our cubicle and begins to ask for prayer for her nephew that got shot in a hold up and then proceeds to mention that the pastor was seen at the hotel with his mistress of 3 years and that Mother Letson is getting put out of her rent controlled apartment cause she has a gambling problem. Just before she leaves she happens to mention how God moved on yesterday and begins bringing up how hard it must be for me to let go of how Jimmy left me and those kids. How she couldn't have made it and how big of a fool he made of me. I had planned to spend some time with the Lord via his word, but my spirit is so heavy by the time she turns me loose until I just reach for my purse and head to my usual retreats the candy machine or the cigarette deck(I'm glad I didn't leave those at the altar like the spirit unctioned me)

Well the the nine has met the five and it's time for me to head home. When I get in the parking lot Bob from accounting has blocked me in for the fourth time and I realize that I still have to get fuel before I head home. I sit and brood and think all kinds of expletives and what I would do if I wasn't saved. By the time he gets out of there, I am so mad until I am cussing. I cuss and talk under my breathe all the way home…oh but wait…I don't quite make it home because I was so busy stewing at Bob until I drove right by the gas station… so on and so forth. Before you know it, I have given up and settled back into my old groove of failing. Only that groove has been knocked

out and reshaped so I can't go backwards...
WHAT DO I DO NOW?

The answer to that question and anymore like it is something different. Insanity is defined as doing the same thing and expecting different results. You cannot rightfully plant lemon seeds and expect a peach orchard. Your expectation of fruit and yield is off. Planting and reaping are not foreign concepts to each other. Seeds, fertilizer, water and cultivation make for a fine harvest, but it takes ALL of them to produce. Do not expect to take only the seeds or to devour the dung as food. We can survive on water, but there are some nutrients that can only be ingested from plant life.

So it is in the spiritual. The seeds that are planted in our hearts on Sundays, Tuesdays or Wednesday night bible classes are not designed to be our complete sustenance. It takes the cultivation of trials, putrid potency of fertilizer and the water of experience to make the harvest that is called us. We want to take one over the other, thinking that any stage in our growth is bad. My friend it is anything but! If I must say so myself… everything God created was good.

Mental breakdowns:

We are going to look at a concept of disruption that has been a thorn in the side of the promised people since the exodus from Egypt. In Numbers 16, we see where this small group of 250 plus women and children that caused a mighty rift in the unity and harmony of God's people. The rebellion of Kora, can teach us many lessons. However, I am only going to focus on one in this book: The lesson of the clouded perception.

Kora no doubt felt because he could articulate better than Moses that he was a more qualified candidate for the position to be the go-between God and the Hebrews. "You take too much upon yourselves..." he chided Moses and Aaron. We could make the assumption and say he was jealous because Moses was showing favoritism to his brother. We would be wrong because Kora was Moses' cousin. What exactly was his reasoning? What gave him the right to make these statements? In all honesty, Kora had every right to make these assessments. He was absolutely right. He was a Levite or a priest as a matter of fact so were Datham, and Abiram and the other 250 men were as well. They were no doubt well versed in democratic assemblies and would have made excellent governors...but God. It wasn't about the people's wish; it was about where God was taking them. They were trying to establish themselves, but God was trying to do it without man's assistance. He had other plans for them, but they were so busy helping Him out until they couldn't see that His plan required only their devotion and obedience.

Kora talked himself Datham, Abiram 250 men with their wives and children into a fiery grave. God made examples out of them. He was making it clear to the entire nation that it all was His decision. He was calling the shots and it will be His way or suffer the consequences. So in essence, God was doing a cleansing. In the lineage of Kora and the rest there is rumored to Egyptian blood. It was God's desire that the nation of Israel remain pure. They had intermarried with other nations and had other allegiances. This was not acceptable in God's destiny. Their only allegiance was to be to the one and only God Jehovah.

Also, it is possible that the ones who perished in Kora's shenanigans were sent along by the Egyptians to sabotage the Children of Israel's journey. You could say this little stunt was also a way to weed out the weeds. I am by no means saying our God is prejudice or biased, but He wanted to make a complex example of the children into a simple lesson of acceptance for us. See everything in the bible is about Calvary. Everyone else was grafted into the family of the Hebrews via Jesus, but we all have the same promises as Abraham and all of His heirs. The adopted sons have the same lot as the born sons.

<u>The Rabble</u>
Noun: an angry mob or disorganization, clutter

History tells us that Kora was no ordinary troublemaker, he was well versed in the temple rites as a matter of fact he is a descendant of the tribe of Benjamin. He was Moses' cousin so the enemy in this case was a man of his own household.

How many times have we ruled out our surroundings as the very thing that is stunting our growth? Are you aware of how much trouble an earthworm can cause a plant? It will drain all the nutrients from the soil and cause a malnourished plant to dry up at the source of its intake...the roots. If the roots are not getting enough water and fertilizer then the leaves will begin to die and no sunlight is being absorbed. If no sunlight is absorbed then no oxygen can be released and no oxygen can be released, the process of photo-synthesis cannot process then the life of the plant ceases.

It happened the same way with the children of Israel. Kora was a hindrance it's true, but he was stopped before he could cause death to the life of the tree. I would like to look at the cleansing God did when He chastised the rabble. When a metal is in its purest form, that's when it is most adaptable.

Verb: the actual puddling as in a refinery producing fine metals

*puddling: the method of converting pig iron into wrought by subjecting it to heat and frequent stirring

When we apply this to our own growth and development this is how it will look:

1. Remove people from your life that are toxic.

a) Gossipers   b) liars/talebearers
c) negative   d) past hurts

2. Get your life in order:

a) Time management
b) money management
c) spiritual management
2a) Prepare for the unexpected/prepare to win instead of lose
2b) Budget and give accordingly
2c) Daily dose of vitamin "B" (the bible)

Maintains metabolism: sustains the functions of life rebuilding and detoxing of tissues

Maintains muscle tone or strength

*We experience triumphs not trials. The difficulties we experience are for the purpose of strength training. Our endurance and stamina are built by the things we go thru.

Enhance immunity to carnal thinking and reaction (nervous system)

Promotes growth in red blood cells that prevent spiritual anemia (decreased number of red blood cells, that decreases the amount of oxygen (Holy Ghost influence) in our decision making

Scriptures:

Exodus 14, 15, 16 the entire history of the rebellion

Song of Solomon 2:15 take us the little foxes, the little foxes that spoil the vines: for our vines have tender grapes.

Romans 5:3-5

*Glory in tribulations for they are our strength.

Proverbs 3:11-12

* My son despise not the chastening of the Lord; neither be weary of his correction

2 Corinthians 12:7-10

*Paul's thorn in the flesh.

Mind
(The Playing Field)

"As a man thinketh in his heart so is he." Carnality is a disconnection in communication with God. This is why it is his enemy. It makes the believer act contrary to what His will is. Everything God created was for our good and His glory. Those things can't rightfully be unless we are on the same page as Him. If you aren't with me you are automatically against. There is no in between…it either is or it isn't.

The reason carnality is so lethal is because it entertains us while wait for promises due us by God to be fulfilled. This may not be a bad idea for a child to learn to entertain his or herself…but what if they were playing with an electrical cord? Yes they will have found a way to occupy their time, but what they are occupying it with is very dangerous and could destroy them.

So it is with carnality my friends. Carnality is a live wire with no insulation that will burn all your hopes and dreams up and terminate any promises for the future. Those vivid images we create put us in a position of Lordship. We have established our interest and what we want out of the situation, and begin to perform our lives according to those guidelines we have set forth for ourselves. This imaginary audience will judge us, inform us, instruct us and correct us all according to our own selfish desires.

Don't get me wrong, self chastisement as described in I Corinthians 11:3 will carry us a long way, but to live each day inside our own head keeps us from enjoying the real life God has planned for us. In doing so, we limit and distract ourselves from the true purpose of what God made those promises for in the beginning.

In all actuality, REALITY is the biggest,

baddest rollercoaster ride in the amusement park of life and carnality is that loooooong line that prolongs your wait for the ride. Notice I didn't say that it keeps you from the ride. No weapon, not even the ones we have created ourselves shall prosper.

The real problem with our carnal view is we are short sided and cannot see as far as the real God and can miss some key points. Nothing we do is for ourselves. We are all connected somehow, in some way, in some form or another. My life affects someone else's and someone else's life is a pattern for me and so on and so forth. By leaving all the details to God we are relinquishing our responsibility and are finally able to live the fantastic life we were given way back in the garden.

We ask God for strength and when a situation comes where we have to be strong, we pray for Him to remove it. Likewise when we ask for joy, healing, financial blessings, more anointing, or a closer walk, God will put us in situations to exercise what He has already placed on the inside of us. It takes practice to go from 1-lb to 100lb, so it is in the spirit realm. We must learn skill in our gifts…well first we must learn what our gifts are and THEN we look for practice scenarios.

Please don't think that the ides of our imagination are limited to how we view our situations. We can also be held captive to a poor image of whom or what people really are. No one is as "good" or as "bad" as they are made out to be. We must learn to examine people from our first hand knowledge of their spiritual energy. Even the human propensities are a mask covering our true identity.

When we give in to the secret lust of carnality or subversion, we set ourselves up for the ultimate okey-doke. We not only bring down our own standards of living, but we misrepresent what the scriptures have been passing down thru generations. This is commonly known as subversion. Prophetess what is subversion you ask… well I will tell you.

Subvert:

To overthrow or destroy
something established

To corrupt, as in morals

Ways to subvert or be guilty of subversion:

1. **Pride-Daniel 4:1-37**: <u>God chooses
   whomever He will</u>-This is the lesson
   we learn from this passage. Poor
   King Nebuchadnezzar. He didn't
   even see it coming. He was looking
   the wrong way when fate fell on
   him. That is our problem as well.
   We seek in the wrong direction
   for directions, because our eyes are
   full of our own agendas. There is a
   way that seems right to man, but
   in the end thereof is death. In this
   king's case it was insanity. He had
   a nervous breakdown. I too have
   been the victim of my own ego.
   I separated myself from everyone
   that I loved, even though I was

not sure if they loved me. I wanted to make an impact on the world but I was just making skid marks. Anxiety kicked my butt! The whole purpose of my having a ministry, a business, and financial stability is so I can build the kingdom.

2. **Disobedience-Jonah2:1-9 -** <u>The example of what not to do</u>- Jonah blatantly disobeyed God and when the storms of life caught up to him, he bailed out. Even in his cowardice approach to his mission, he knew that God would not abandon him. He chided the men on board the ship to throw him overboard, because there in the turbulence of the storm, was his vindication. We could look at this in two ways: 1. Jonah knew his life would not end until his purpose was complete and 2. No matter what mess we get ourselves into, God always provides an out.

However, in this lesson we will simply say that in order to create a more effective minister, God teaches by way of example. The all knowing God we serve knew Jonah would run when He called him, that's why He let him. Jonah got himself into the same predicament of disobedience and rebellion that this people were accused of. He carefully led Jonah to the ocean where met the ultimate teacher in nature. While the seaweed was wrapped around Jonah's head, he had the chance to see the bottom of the mountains. He sank to depths he had never known and experienced pressures he never knew he could survive. Without all of these experiences, Jonah never would have developed the passion for his mission. Once the scenic route was over, it was time to go to work. He took a 3 day journey and made it in 1. Some use this as a preaching tool to say this was a reward, but not necessarily. Jonah had wasted time and the people he was supposed to reach, needed to hear the word from the Lord. They were perishing and there was no time to waste. Once he arrived in Nineveh, he began crying out like never before. He ministered with such conviction even the king took heed and called for a governmental fast. He declared that everyone examine their ways and turn back to God. Mission complete. Jonah was successful and God had His people back. All should have been well, but our little carnal friend Jonah went and sat under a bush and waited for the destruction that had been thwarted by their obedience. He began to whine to God and say "See…this is why I didn't want to come and do this.

Now everybody thinks I'm a false prophet. Nothing happened!" God being the loving father He is, put the big baby down for a nap and while he was sleeping, caused a gourd to grow up around him. When he awakened he took notice to the plant, and saw where the sun was drying it out. Jonah took pity on the gourd and began to worry about its survival. God explained to Jonah that just as he had compassion for that gourd, He had compassion for the people of Nineveh.

3. Bitterness-Isaiah 1:5-6 – <u>Being governed by emotions</u> – When the head is sick, the whole body is corrupted. When an opportunity to forgive and release is presented, there is a gnawing, jaw clenching urge to hold the offender accountable for their deeds. In all actuality at this point we have

traded places with our bullies and are responding in the same spirit with which we have been offended. It is a prison designed to keep us housed and stifled. The most effective weapon against bitterness is forgiveness. This tool is very seldom used in the reconstruction of one's psyche, yet it is the only one that will ensure complete restoration.

4. Idolatry-II Chronicles 26:1 _ Uzziah decided that he would take on the job of the priests. The 5verse states that as long as he sought the Lord, God made him to prosper. That is another problem with carnality; it causes one to stop seeking God. We turn inward and listen to the selfish voice that would put our finite judgment over the infinite soundness of God's. We will see things as "we" think they are and not as they

truly are. Carnality is equivalent to an alcohol stupor that makes someone fairly unattractive appear totally acceptable. Isaiah 6:1 states that the year Uzi died I saw the Lord and he was high and lifted up and his train filled the temple. This is argued that after Uzziah, a king who became leprous as a result of his ego died, a vision of the messiah was seen by the prophet. Let's concentrate on the basics of this statement. After ego dies, we can see the most High. God can rightfully take his place in our minds when we die of our own devices.

5. Jealousy- I Samuel 18:6-11- Samuel had lost his natural mind for thinking that he could disobey a vow of appointment and still remain God's chosen king. Even in reading the passages about his demise, you can see that his

jealousy was not because he still wanted to be king, but God's favor had left him and he was no longer in the spotlight. His emulation was so strong that even when the anointed psalmist David tried to play and soothe his mind, it only angered him more. So much so that it caused him to try and spear David with a javelin. This is a testimony of how deeply rooted jealousy can be. It will try to destroy the very entity of help so it can prevail.

6. Losing Focus- I Kings 19:4-8- The great prophet Elijah who chastised Jezebel and the prophets of Baal. The man who was raptured away and never tasted death. He was also one of the figures seen on the mount of transfiguration with Jesus, was also one of the weakest minds to grace the presence of the earth. His life is a testament of being

able to do great works in God's strength, but still being subject to the finiteness of humanity. In this passage he was battling depression and feeling inadequate. The fact of the matter is we are inadequate and finite and subject to all of the ides of the flesh. We cannot save what is unsalvageable. We must remember that any acts of ability are done through us by God not the other way around. In those times of vulnerability, we should exercise the art of being still and quiet. This is the proper attitude of how to wait on God so that He can guide us into our next mission.

7. Lying- Acts 5:1-11- What was Ananias and Sapphira thinking? We could easily say because he was the head of the household, he should have been accountable. Well in the old testament, before grace and Calvary that would have been

the case. Look at Adam and Eve. Their death did not come about until HE ate of the tree. Let's take the example of Kora and the crew. The passage said 250 men and then women and children perished. Here we could see these two as a parable of the new Adam and Eve. It was his idea, but she could have saved herself. The apostles spoke to each separately about the amount of money they received for a possession. Had she told the truth, she would have been spared. We are no longer bound to the law, but to the Holy Ghost. Peter made it explicitly clear that the lie was not told to man, but to the spirit and that they were now subject to the appropriate consequence. You may not fall dead, but every time you put your own agenda before that of the Holy Spirit, you die a little in your mind.

Third Eye
(Audience of One)

Who are you performing for?

When you are going about daily deeds, who do you think is watching you?

Are you the center of attention in your own head or are you the star of a one man stage play for all who will occupy the audience?

I ask these questions because we all believe that someone is watching us. We will not smoke or drink or even say certain words because we fear that one of the chosen frozen will see us and pass judgment. Never mind that it may ruin a witness or cause our brother to stumble, but we don't want Mother so-and so to see us and be disappointed. We wear our dresses to the floor and ¾ sleeves on our blouses because it makes us look sanctified. We even learn the latest worship songs and practice the proper time to cry and quicken so that we seem deep and spirit filled. If you ask me there are more actors in any edifice than there are at the Oscars.

Don't get me wrong, there are some people who take their walk with God very seriously, but the one who are just playing church have given these few a bad reputation.

Some ailing souls will never get the help they need because of a bad experience they had with a church. I have come to bring a bit of good news to those hurting and even to the one perpetrating the fraud.

Habakkuk 2:1-3 mentions a type of pest that has been misunderstood. The locust has been deemed a plague and rightfully so. It has been destroying crops for many millenniums and today it is a detriment to the spiritual harvest.

Let's look at the various stages of its development in the form of the people we may meet in the church. The first stage mentioned is the gnawing locust. This stage is just after it is born. This can be likened unto a new convert. They are very young spiritually and at best are just talebearers and backbiters who are full of negativity and are most effective against other babes and sucklings who don't know enough word to combat the attacks so they wither in zealousness.

The next stage of the locust is a flying one. This, my friends is a renegade spirit that flits from one church to another under the spirit of evangelism. In all actuality they are angered by something that does not go their way, so they leave and try to start over somewhere else only to end up leaving again when things don't go their way.

Thirdly, is the licking locust. This one is the most venomous because it leaves behind a spiritual residue that corrodes. This is a witch. This spirit will tell lies and spin stories that may even make the truth seem a bit weak. Witchcraft is not a pot with various entrails and herbs boiling over an open fire, but poisonous words that interfere with one's ability to see clearly and think logically.

Lastly, is the full grown locust. This is that mother or deacon that has been holding down traditions so long that they are stifling the growth of the church. They sit down young mothers or shoot down play ideas because they may seem too fast. These are reprobate saints. They have no idea what godliness is, yet the claim that they speak on his behalf. They sit on the phone daily with their bibles on their laps talking down the word while they pass judgment and placate holiness. These are the most dangerous, because most will live to please them and forget that it is all about pleasing God.

Printed in the United States
By Bookmasters